Clas...
Volume Seven

Volkswagen
Transporter
1950-1990

Richard Copping

Nostalgia Road Publications

CONTENTS

The Nostalgia Road Series™

is produced under licence by

Nostalgia Road Publications Ltd.
Units 5-8, Chancel Place, Shap Road Industrial Estate,
Kendal, Cumbria, LA9 6NZ
Tel: +44(0)1539 738832 - Fax: +44(0)1539 730075

designed and published by

Trans-Pennine Publishing Ltd.
PO Box 10, Appleby-in-Westmorland, Cumbria, CA16 6FA
Tel: +44(0)17683 51053 Fax: +44(0)017683 53558
e-mail:admin@transpenninepublishing.co.uk

and printed by
Kent Valley Colour Printers Ltd.
Kendal, Cumbria. Tel: +44(0)1539 741344

© Text: Trans-Pennine Publishing Ltd. 2005
© Photographs Ken Cservenka, or as credited
Archive material – author's collection

Front Cover: *This Panel, or Delivery van, dates from 1956 and is one of 22,657 such models produced that year. It is finished in Dove Blue, a shade that was introduced at the start of Transporter production and remained an option to the end of first-generation production in July 1967.*

Rear Cover Top: *The new generation of Transporters, launched in August 1967, only had one major facelift in nearly 12-years of production. The Panel van depicted is a post-July 1972 model and demonstrates the concept's versatility, in this instance performing the role of a disaster support vehicle.*

Rear Cover Bottom: *The third-generation of Transporter, launched in 1979, retained an air-cooled, rear-mounted, engine against the odds. However, in 1982, a water-cooled boxer engine was introduced. The popular double-cab Pickup option illustrated, features this engine, the telltale second front grille being the giveaway.*

Title Page: *VW's Transporter. From Panel Van to Pickup, Kombi to Microbus, versatility was the key to sales success.*

This Page: *Total production of the second-generation Transporter amounted to nearly 2.5 million vehicles, easily outselling its predecessor's 1.8-million run over a greater number of years. However, other manufacturers were catching up and the third generation model didn't produce such excellent figures.*

INTRODUCTION

November 1949 saw the press launch of a vehicle that was to revolutionise the world of the light commercial. This was the Volkswagen Transporter, now invariably referred to as the 'Splittie', thanks to its 'split' front-screen. From Panelvan, to Kombi and multi-windowed Microbus Deluxe, soon to be supplemented by Pickups and even high top models, here was something unprecedented. The ground-rules for the Transporter's versatility was demonstrably complete. For 17-years, first the VW plant at Wolfsburg and later a purpose-built factory at Hanover, produced the vehicle that was designated simply as the Type 2 Transporter by its creators: a move intended to distinguish it from the Type 1, or Beetle. A staggering 1,833,000 Splitties were built until the model was superseded in August 1967.

Thanks to its panoramic front screen, the nickname for the second-incarnation of the Transporter, produced until 1979, is the Bay. Despite some initial diehard reservations, the Bay had achieved its own cult status by the end of the 1960s and, over its 12-year production run, an additional 2,465,000 Transporters were notched up. The Emden plant, originally conceived to build Beetles for the USA, supplemented Hanover's endeavours. Where the Splittie had led, the Bay followed, pushing away further barriers in the process.

The third design of Transporter (production started in May 1979), still carried the traditional flat-four air-cooled engine. A larger vehicle than its predecessors and officially designated the Type 25, it soon became known as the 'Wedge'. The air-cooled era finally came to an end in 1982. Inevitably, some refused to countenance the change, while, thanks to the emergence of a string of products from rival manufacturers, VW started to lose its vice-like grip on the smaller commercial vehicle market. The Type 25 represented the Transporter when VW celebrated the product's 40th anniversary on March 8th 1990, but six-months later the fourth-generation was launched, providing an appropriate cut-off point for this volume.

This is the 40-year tale of three-generations of Transporter, peppered with pictures and descriptions of the largely 'semi-unofficial' but popular Camper conversions, set against the knowledge that nowadays VW enthusiasts see all models as appreciating assets. From the days when the T25 was scorned as just an old and decidedly undesirable VW and the Bay played a very second fiddle to the invincible Splittie, to shows packed from wall to wall with the products of Volkswagen's honest labours, it's an honour to put pen to paper in pursuit of their respective stories.

Richard Copping

Kirkby Lonsdale
September 2005

Birth of a Concept

Three factors led to the creation of the Volkswagen Transporter as we know it today. The first was the ingenuity of the Senior Resident Officer in the immediate post-war period at the former Nazi-owned factory. The second was the arrival on the scene of an extrovert Dutchman, with an eye for making a quick buck. The third can be rested at the door of a former Opel truck division Director, who was to build Volkswagen into a multi-million Deutsche-mark business within a few short years.

Although the Beetle's creator, Ferdinand Porsche, had produced more than a summary sketch of various vehicles primarily to carry goods rather than people, the intervention of war was to scupper any such notions. Porsche became involved in projects designed to secure Germany's good fortunes in the conflict. Meanwhile, modified Beetles, with the equivalent of garden sheds on their backs, were the Nazi era's best effort!

Above: *The Plattenwagen, or flatbed warehouse truck, created by Ivan Hirst due to the departure of suitable trucks from Wolfsburg, was the key inspiration behind the VW Transporter.*

The story of Yorkshireman, Major Ivan Hirst's arrival at Wolfsburg, with no specific orders other than to take control, is well known. *Ad hoc* ingenuity soon became synonymous with the Major's name and it was his ability to rapidly resolve problems that eventually led to the creation of the VW Transporter. When the heavy engineering unit and their attendant flotilla of trucks left Wolfsburg in 1946, Hirst had to think on his feet. His solution, was the Plattenwagen; literally a flatbed truck cobbled together from bits of Beetles, most notably the running gear and the wartime Kübelwagen. The small band of practical, but hardly elegant, 'Plattenwagens' enjoyed a lengthy existence as an essential part of VW factory life, with the last one only being pensioned off as recently as 1994.

The name of Dutchman Ben Pon is one of the best known in relation to the early days of the VW story. Accompanied by his brother Wijnand, he had established contact with the Nazis as early as 1937 with a view to selling the Volkswagen in his native Netherlands. After the war in 1946, and temporarily 'commissioned' a full Colonel, Pon decorated his chest with a series of phoney medals, 'hired' a chauffeur and made his way to Wolfsburg in an old Mercedes. His intention was to impress the British and perchance gain the 'franchise' he had sought previously. Although this visit ended in nothing, Pon persisted, his name eventually coming to the attention of Colonel Radclyffe, head of light mechanical engineering at the industry division of the Military Government based at Minden. After meetings between the two men, on 8th August 1947 a contract was signed between the Volkswagenwerk and Pon's Automobielhandel. Once an Opel agent, Pon became the first authorised importer of Beetles anywhere in Europe and beyond, although it was October 1947 before he eventually acquired his first 'new' Beetles.

With the aid of hired drivers, Pon relayed them back to his hometown of Amersfoort in Holland. Clearly, by this time his credibility was firmly established. One Royal Mechanical & Electrical Engineer inspection team member recalled Pon's visits to Wolfsburg well. Apart from expressing a great interest in issues of quality, his observations invariably seemed to concern 'developments', while he was remembered as being 'always full of life'. Thanks to that fertile imagination and an eye for business, when Pon spotted Hirst's Plattenwagen, he attempted to get it certified as street legal in the Netherlands. The authorities decreed that the driver must be seated at the front and Pon's initial plan was thwarted. However, as a logical development of the Plattenwagen scheme, at a meeting with Hirst on 23rd April 1947, Pon sketched a box-like commercial vehicle, remarkably similar in appearance to what the world would later recognise as the first VW Transporter.

Below: *A Volkswagen publicity shot dating from 1953. A rear bumper would be added to the 1954 model year specification.*

Top Left: *In the early months of production, the Transporter lacked any form of rear window, but the large VW roundel was discontinued in November 1950.*

Bottom Left: *Noticeable in this view is the enormous engine lid, which has since been christened the 'barn door' by the VW fraternity. There was no access to the interior of the model from the rear and nor would there be until a re-design in March 1955. Early Transporters also lacked a rear bumper.*

Pon's sketch depicted a rear engined van with the driver positioned over the front wheels. The engine was accessed via an upward opening tailgate, while the box-shaped body was capable of carrying up to 750kg. Although the equally imaginative Hirst was impressed, when the 'design' was put before Radclyffe he argued, with some justification, that the factory was already stretched to capacity in its quest to meet demand for the saloon.

Heinz Nordhoff was appointed General Director of Volkswagen with effect from 1st January 1948, a post he would hold until his death in April 1968. By 1948 plans were already in hand for the British Military Government to gradually withdraw from German soil and this one-time Director of the Opel plant in Brandenburg, the largest truck factory in pre-war Europe, was seen as an ideal candidate to take control at Wolfsburg. Although perhaps not innovative like Porsche, his autocratic determination for VW to succeed, his grounding in US methods of production and his incredible organisational skills, were exactly what was required.

Nordhoff would make use of Ben Pon in his quest to take the Beetle to the United States and it seems more than likely that the Dutchman presented his ideas for a commercial vehicle at the earliest opportunity. Hirst's role is unclear, but as Nordhoff had insisted that he wanted no interference from the British, it seems probable that it was Pon alone who met with an enthusiastic Nordhoff. By the autumn of 1948, the decision had been made to proceed with such a vehicle. Conceivably currency reform and the introduction of the Deutsch-mark in June 1948, which heralded the end of the short supply economy, was the catalyst Nordhoff needed. Beetle production escalated from 1,185 units in May, to 2,306 by the end of the year, while Alfred Haesner, the factory's Technical Director, got the go-ahead to start plan EA-7, Development Project No7 – the Transporter. Nordhoff's brief for his self-designated 'box on wheels' was that all preconceived ideas of what a delivery van should contain must be ignored.

By 20th November 1948, two Transporter designs had been presented: one with a straight, flat driver's cab, which was rejected and a second, with a slightly raked front, that was given the go-ahead. Inevitably, in a laudable attempt to save money, as many Beetle parts as possible were utilised. Hence, the car's 25hp engine was positioned at the rear of the new vehicle, while the standard VW crash-box was bolted directly to it. The first Transporter was completed on 9th March 1949, but testing had to be halted some three weeks later on 5th April.

Sadly, the widened, but otherwise unmodified, Beetle chassis was totally unsuited to its new task. It was not strong enough to withstand the increased stresses, twisting and folding when weight was placed in the load carrying section. Haesner reported that "the passenger vehicle chassis" couldn't perform the tasks required of it "for the load and the torsion in particular, is simply too great". The design department set about rebuilding the first prototype and added a second, featuring what was essentially a unitary design, with two hefty longitudinal members and robust supporting outriggers. Amazingly, tests recommenced in May, although it was clear by this time that the new VW supremo Heinz Nordhoff was at his most demanding.

On 19th May, Nordhoff decreed that production of the Transporter would begin in November 1949, with an absolute deadline of December, so that the new model could be delivered at the beginning of 1950. A reduction drive, similar to that of the Kübelwagen, gave greater transmission ratio and better ground clearance, while cost-saving dual torsion springs were used for the back axle. The prototype was subjected to 12,000km of testing over the worst roads possible and passed with flying colours, although plans to test it on a hill at the north curve on the Nurbürgring had to be abandoned, due to lack of time.

Top Right: *All split-screen Transporters benefited from easy side access, thanks to double doors. Later a sliding door was an option, but it was never a standard part of the first-generation Transporter package. Loading doors were standard on the driver's side of the vehicle, although it wasn't long before they could be specified on both sides at extra cost.*

Bottom Right: *Behind the 'barn door' was a cavernous space housing the diminutive 25bhp engine 'borrowed' from the Beetle, a precariously balanced fuel tank and a vertically stored spare wheel. The spare wheel was re-located to a position above the engine in 1951, a move that also divided the fuel tank filler from direct contact with the engine …phew!*

Above: *From the start, Volkswagen advertised the Panelvan as providing a canvas to promote businesses.*

In August 1949, the decision was taken to produce four more prototypes covering the different model types envisaged. These included a straightforward Panelvan, a Pickup and an eight-seat Microbus. Everything was to be ready by 15th October. Nordhoff took a deep interest in the programme, suggesting improvements, and a fifth second-generation prototype was commissioned as a result.

On 12th November, the Transporter was presented to the press. Nordhoff stressed that the lack of a name was its only defect. The Transporter would be built without 'compromises'. "This is why we did not start from an available chassis, but from the cargo space", he said. "With this van, and only this van, the cargo space lies exactly between the axles. The driver sits in the front and there is equal weight in the back, due to the fuel tank and engine; that is the best compromise". He summarised the Transporter as a, "combination of a unitised body, with the main characteristics of a Volkswagen".

The first Transporters trickled off the assembly line in February 1950, for use as test vehicles of VW's most important customers. The vehicle officially went on sale when it was launched at the Geneva Motor Show in March, and on the 8th of that month full-scale production was started, at a rate of 10-vehicles daily.

Nowadays, most authors insist that the Transporter was an instant success and production of 8,059 vehicles in the first year would seem to confirm this. However, while Nordhoff told everyone that here was a vehicle that would, "revolutionise the truck industry", Volkswagen was later to admit that "the reception that greeted the …[vehicles on display at Geneva] … was slightly less than spectacular". In fact, the truck world viewed the project with scepticism.

By the 1960s, a knowledgeable writer on the subject could state of the Transporter that Nordhoff "blazed a trail, one which would eventually be followed by other manufacturers ...". At 5,850DM when launched there was little available as an alternative in the same price-bracket. "The famous cab above the engine design gave such horrendous loading characteristics that we never even considered it", said Nordhoff. "You can tell by the trees in the British zone how well the army lorries, built with this principle, handle on wet roads when they are not loaded".

In Germany, reliance had been placed on two-stroke engines often coupled to a three-wheel combination. In Britain the best vehicle on offer was the Morris J-type van, while in France Citroen were contemplating the most basic of vehicles, the Type H van, consisting of 'corrugated' panels and front-wheel drive. Soon VW came to dominate not only in Europe, but also across the world and especially in the USA.

As the years passed by, Volkswagen had to fight harder as more manufacturers endeavoured to emulate the Transporter. In Britain BMC, Commer and Bedford brought out alternatives; while in the USA the likes of Chevrolet, with their Greenbier, replicated the drive-train layout but offered a useful 2377cc flat six engine. Ford presented the Econoline, an easy to load vehicle, thanks to its low rear platform, while in Europe, both Fiat (and their Multipla) and Renault (with the Estafette), were able to sell sufficient quantities to become common sights on the roads. Even so, the Transporter was a great success story for Nordhoff. By 1959 production had risen to 121,453, and peaked at 187,947 vehicles in 1964.

Below: *The keeper of this early Panelvan owned a Volkswagen dealership in Bad Camberg, Germany. While his business was selling new VWs, he could also advertise his passion in time-honoured fashion.*

THE RANGE OF TRANSPORTERS

Although the Panelvan was the first variant of the Transporter to be launched, the previously outlined prototype production indicated that the intention was always to present buyers with a whole range of vehicles, designed for a variety of purposes. In chronological sequence, each Transporter option is now described, making use of Volkswagen's own somewhat turgid writings, typical of the age, thankfully accompanied by the delightful artwork of Bernd Reuters. The artist exaggerated the Transporter's lines, emphasising styling details, which in turn made the 'box on wheels' thoroughly expressive.

The Panel, or Delivery Van, was initially offered in just glossy Dove Blue finish, or simple primer. Of the 4,345 panel vans built in the first year, nearly 46% were delivered in the latter option, so that purchasers could add their company livery. This led VW to exploit the advertising potential of the Transporter in its most basic form. "The Volkswagen Delivery Van has large smooth panels ideal for advertising. They can be made into travelling signboards that are the cheapest but most effective advertising you can give your firm". This message was also expressed in a more flowing manner. "Painted in your firm's colours … the Volkswagen Delivery Van is excellent publicity for your firm. Its trim modern lines and the slick way it slips through traffic attracts the eye of the public. The name of your firm is shown to full advantage on the large flat panels. The sight of the ultra modern Volkswagen shows the public: a Volkswagen owner is on his toes!"

Bearing in mind that until 1955 there was no rearward access to the interior and even then it was restricted, Volkswagen had to sell the public an alternative story. "It is easy to load even the bulkiest goods through the spacious double side doors. The large floor of the vehicle is just a few inches above the pavement and it is flat like a table. You can stand in the doorway and reach every corner of the vehicle, thus avoiding all that running back and forth so necessary in rear-loading vans".

Top Left: *Compare this 1950 Panelvan with the one illustrated top right on page 11. The giant VW symbol was discontinued in November 1950, but it wasn't until April 1951 that a rear window was added.*

Bottom Left: *From the front the Panelvan was distinctive, and was made more so by the prominent usage of the VW logo; a feature that remained intact throughout the first generation's production run.*

Top Right: *Although this 'barn door' Panelvan has been lowered and fitted with wheels incorrect for all years, it serves to illustrate the arrival of a not unusually small rear window.*

Middle Right: *Hinged side doors were standard throughout the Splittie's production run.*

Bottom Right: *Volkswagen always suggested that the Panelvan provided ample 'space' for advertising. It would appear that modern-day owners are still taking their advice!*

Other highlighted features included "the wide unencumbered doors of the cabin", which were "particularly appreciated in delivery work requiring much getting in and out" and the "perfect" weight distribution even when empty, "because the driver is in the front and the engine is in the rear where it ought to be, next to the rear wheels, thus avoiding the need of power wasting drive shafts and bearings".

Volkswagen's message changed little. In 1966 the Delivery Van's economy was still stressed; "VW commercials give you more for less – more profits at less operating costs and more in performance and mileage (powerful 1.5litre engine). More load space too (roomy 1 tonner)". Its roominess was emphasised more than the balance of weight distribution, "VW Delivery Vans can transport all kinds of things … it doesn't matter what. Because the VW Delivery Van has lots of room for everything. It has 170cu.ft of load space and can carry 2,205lbs".

The message of weight distribution was still present. "The load rides in the middle. So your VW Commercial offers you equal weight distribution front and rear. Moreover the weight of the engine on the drive wheels gives better traction". Its manoeuvrability and compact size became the main headline. The VW Delivery Van [has] quick loading", shouted the copywriter, before continuing that "the VW Commercial is just as fleet and nimble as the Volkswagen itself (it's only 9-inches longer)".

In 1950 the Delivery Van accounted for a little over 70% of all Transporter sales, not a surprise as other variants only started to emerge as the year went by. By 1953, numbers had dropped to a more realistic 40% although with the dawning of the new decade, the norm settled at a percentage in the late 20s. In comparison with vans of more recent times, the Delivery Van was Spartan in the extreme but, compared to its contemporaries, it is little wonder that it was a tremendous success story for Volkswagen.

The Kombi Station Wagon

Handsome outside, and inside:
nine seats or 170 cubic feet
— at your service for business and pleasure.

Top, Middle and Bottom Left: *"Handsome outside and inside: nine seats or 170 cubic feet – at your service for business and pleasure. The Kombi Station Wagon". So ran the text to accompany the artwork reproduced top left. Clever but undoubtedly basic, as the lack of trim and door cards, plus acres of bare painted metal serves to illustrate (middle left). The use of wing nuts (Bottom left) as a means to remove the rear compartment seats was positively primitive. As can be imagined, in case of an accident, this kind of design hardly provided an adequate mounting device on a passenger seat, for under extreme pressure the seat could move or even become free.*

Hot on the heels of the Delivery Van, came the Kombi and the Microbus, both of which were officially launched in June 1950. The addition of three-rectangular windows, on each side of both vehicles, immediately distinguished them from the 'slab' sided Delivery van. The first Kombi, delivered in primer, pre-empted its official debut by a few weeks, having been built as early as May 13th. Full-scale production of the Microbus started on May 22nd.

The Kombi was unquestionably the world's first true multi-purpose vehicle and Volkswagen's copywriters were quick to explain its versatility. "Take out the seats and it is an efficient delivery van suitable for quick delivery service of any kind. ... Put the roomy well-cushioned seats into the Volkswagen Kombi and it is a comfortable passenger vehicle seating eight".

Although passengers seated in what doubled as a loading area were afforded a rubber mat on which to put their feet, complimenting more of the same in the cab, the Kombi followed to the letter the accoutrements of the Delivery Van in the 'cargo' area. As such, it lacked a headlining for the five passengers not sat in the cab, while the interior remained un-panelled, affording less than stimulating views of acres of painted metal. Luxury evaded the driver and his front seat companions too for, while there was both a headlining and door cards, each was made of plain fibreboard. Unlike many Export Beetles with cloth upholstery, at least in the early to mid-1950s, the Kombi was always upholstered in Vinyl, while until 1963, when the driver acquired his own separate front seat, the bench-seat couldn't be adjusted. Like the Standard model Beetle, the load area seats were secured by simple wing nuts.

Fortunately, unlike the Delivery Van's dividing 'wall' between the cab and the loading section, the Kombi had a cut-down panel, while from 1953 there was an option to specify a walkway from the cab.

"The Volkswagen Kombi – the Combination Van and Bus – … Eight side windows and the large panoramic front window make the interior bright and cheerful. Every passenger has room to spare. The seats can be removed in a twinkling … the six side windows can be easily made into as many travelling show windows for your merchandise. It is extremely effective advertising that costs you nothing! The Volkswagen Kombi is in every sense of the word two efficient money-earning vehicles combined in one". This was the message in the early 1950s and it certainly worked. In 1951, Kombi sales accounted for nearly 24% of total production, a position more or less held for the next 16-years, although in 1966 and '67 there was a steady increase in numbers for the Kombi, while the more expensive Microbus total fell back. With economic problems rife in Germany, perhaps the success of the keenly priced Kombi in those years is explained.

Above: *This Kombi dates from September 1963 and is finished in VW Light Grey. The Kombi is not always necessarily easy to distinguish externally from the more expensive Microbus.*

As the 1960s unfurled VW found more uses for the Kombi. "The VW Kombi is three different cars in one. That means you save buying ten wheels, two engines, two transmissions, tax and insurance on two vehicles".. Emphasis was placed on the extent to which the Kombi had acquired added enticements to buy, such as a "large parcel shelf extending the width of the dashboard. A flexible grab handle for the front passenger. Coat hooks in the driver's cab. Padded sun visors. Fully adjustable heating …"; the list was endless. Most interesting of all though was VW's acknowledgement that the Kombi formed an ideal base for camping. "You can even live in a VW Kombi. (Two grown-ups and one child.) Just install VW camping equipment".

"The Volkswagen Microbus is in reality not a bus but an oversize passenger car accommodating eight persons". So wrote the 1950s brochure compiler, creating in the process a forerunner of the people-carriers of today. Although from the spring of 1951 there was a more luxurious version of the Microbus readily available, the emphasis remained on comfort. "The deeply upholstered seats are so well cushioned that travelling hundreds of miles is a pleasure". Certainly one up on the Kombi, the Microbus featured a full-length headlining, which extended around the side windows. For many years made of cloth, when the vinyl revolution hit the world it was changed to white perforated plastic. The interior had both side and door panels, usually finished in two-tone-colours with anodised alloy mouldings separating each shade. Outer passengers were provided with armrests, while extra trim acted as a sound-deadening agent. While the seats on the Kombi were plain single colour affairs, the Microbus had both pleated and piped trim. The rear seats were benches holding three people each, while the central one had a tipping backrest in the area closest to the door.

Although some Microbuses were painted in a single body colour, others flaunted their panels with attractive two-tone paint. By the mid-1960s, VW's copywriters were far more blatant in their promotion of the Microbus as a car. "It's a large family car. Mum, dad, the kids, granny and granddad enjoy a comfortable ride on its well-upholstered seats". Emphasis was placed on the variations in the number of seats possible. A short middle bench version accommodated seven-passengers. Six people radiated in the extra room available with the middle bench missing, while nine little sardines including the driver was maximum for the Microbus.

Below: *Volkswagen released this publicity picture of the Microbus for 'use after March 1955'. Note the 'peak' that now protrudes over the windscreen, the external petrol-filler flap and the nine lower body vents; all of which are hallmarks of the re-vamped Transporter. The paintwork is two-tone, the hubcaps are chromed and there is a glimpse of more luxurious seating.*

The Sondermodell (Special Model) or Microbus Deluxe, which was previewed at the Frankfurt Motor Show in April 1951 and put into full-scale production in June of the same year, reflected Nordhoff's confidence that a resurgent Germany would pay the price demanded for a little luxury. Commonly known as the Samba, the Microbus Deluxe had a number of exclusive features. For a start the interior was much brighter and airier. This was achieved by the creation of an additional window, wedged into each side of the body, increasing the three rectangular panes to four square ones and losing light restricting metalwork in the process. At the back two wraparound windows replaced more metalwork, while four oblong skylights were added on each side of the roof panel. If that wasn't enough, the Samba came complete with a 'Golde' fold-back sunroof as standard.

Chrome and bright-work abounded, as the Samba was the only model in the range to feature chromed hubcaps and a special shiny VW emblem on its front. Attractive combinations of two-tone paintwork were subtly highlighted using chunky polished alloy mouldings. These mouldings sat on the edge of the 'V-shaped' panel on the Samba's front, in addition to similar trim items below the windows and close to the ground (between the wheels) on its sides.

From the start, the Samba's interior boasted a full-length dash; whilst the rest of the range had to cope with little more than a simple pod, until a general re-vamping in 1955. A clock, plus a blanking panel built to accommodate a radio, were housed in the exclusive dash.

The luggage compartment was carpeted and sported both protective chromed rails and rubbing strips, while upholstery throughout was both piped and fluted. The backrest of the seat nearest the doors was both split from the rest and foldable, allowing much easier access for rear seat passengers. Items like the steering wheel, plus controls and knobs were finished in ivory rather than the more basic looking black. Plated ashtrays and an assortment of additional and extended grab handles completed this handsome package.

Top, Middle and Bottom Right: *Compare the specification of the straightforward Microbus (Top Right) to that of the Deluxe, (Middle Right) and from this period brochure it is easy to see why the latter commanded a premium price. It had 23-windows, when the skylights are included, fold-back sunroof, additional bright work and a more luxurious interior. Volkswagen's publicity shot taken after March 1955, (Bottom Right) emphasises the distinctions.*

The driver's area: visibility is ideal and all controls, including those for heating, ventilation and fuel reserve, are close at hand. Utility shelf stretches full width of cabin beneath the translucent panel; both doors have roomy pockets.

Loads of luggage can be carried in the big trunk area. The rear door opens upward and stays in position automatically.

This "X-ray" picture shows the sensible, attractive design of the interior. The wide seats with their comfortable backs and durable leatherette upholstery allow you to relax even on the longest journey. There is plenty of legroom. Attention has been paid even to the smallest details: there is a handy shelf on the partition behind the driver's compartment ... arm-rests cushioned in durable foam rubber ... practical hand rails ... convenient ash trays ... and hooks for clothing. Luggage is stored well out of the passengers' way.

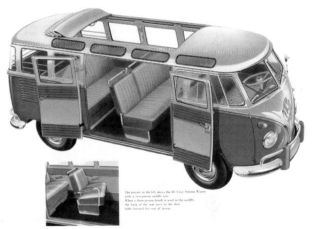

The picture at the left shows the De-Luxe Station Wagon with a two-person middle seat.
When a three-person bench is used in the middle, the back of the seat next to the door folds forward for ease of access.

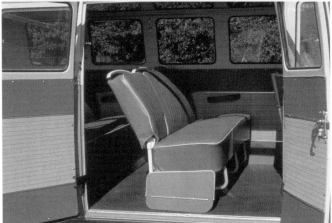

Top, Middle and Bottom Left: *Elegance personified to both then and today, that is VW's Microbus Delux with its abundance of chrome and extra trim. In the 1950s and '60s, two tone paint was far more common, like the Seagull Grey over Mango Green on this 1960 example (Top Left). Meanwhile the attention to aesthetic colour coding of the interior, is revealed Middle Right on a Samba from 1964. Sadly though, when VW increased the Transporter's rearward vision in August 1963, the Deluxe suffered. Gone were the wraparound windows in the rear panels (Bottom Right). The Samba commands 'second-mortgage' prices today, with earlier models in right-hand-drive form being the most sought after.*

Endowed with such a treasure-trove of additional goodies, the copywriters should have had a field day! However, their text was to say the least subtle. "Many leading airlines use this handsome trim Microbus Deluxe to convey passengers to and from the airports" might have been intended to express exclusivity, but to modern eyes the message is lost. Better was the assertion that, "no words or pictures can properly convey to you the beauty, comfort and numerous advantages of this remarkable eight-passenger vehicle". Whilst "Comfortable seats affording each passenger a panoramic view" might have been effective, but "side windows in the roof afford[ing] each passenger an upward view as well", missed the point of this additional design feature.

Although sales of the Samba never rocketed to the levels of some other models in the range, they were always respectable, even when some of its uniqueness was lost. (In 1955 for example 2,195 Sambas were manufactured, compared to 7,957 Microbuses and 11,346 Kombis.) The exclusivity of the dash was lost in 1955, and the addition of a rear bumper in March 1953 was eclipsed when most of the rest of the gang were also so endowed at the end of the year. The two wraparound windows also disappeared in August 1963, when the models all received a much larger rear window in a wider tailgate.

For the 1967 model year VW's brochure writers were happy to list most of what you got for your money with a vehicle that was "even more comfortable and attractive". "Some of the Deluxe features are: sun roof, all round vision, glare absorbing skylights, electric clock on the instrument panel, aluminium rail on back of rear seat bench, eight coat hooks, anodised rim embellishers, anodised waistline mouldings, profile rubber mouldings on the bumpers". Different seat combinations were also highlighted, with an emphasis on walking from the cab to passenger area.

At a time when the Samba was in its infancy, more and more sub-options within the existing Transporter range began to emerge. The Kombi could be specified with a sliding roof, while it was also possible to opt for loading doors on both sides of the Delivery Van. Mumblings of 'Camping Boxes' also started to materialise. In December 1951 VW officially began to produce an ambulance, which for reasons best known to themselves, actually made it as far as inclusion in the pages of their publicity brochures. However, there was still one essential ingredient of the complete Transporter cake missing!

Thanks to the Transporter's success on the market both at home and abroad, Heinz Nordhoff was able to plough profits back into the business,. In turn these funded the reasonably substantial changes required to design and re-tool for a Pickup, the vehicle eventually being launched in August 1952. As the Pickup's bed needed to be flat, the fuel tank had to be both re-sited and re-designed. It was duly relocated to a position above and to the right of the gearbox, a move that necessitated a fuel neck filler on the right hand side of the body, in reality a better position than of old.

The spare wheel was also moved, this time from a horizontal position above the engine, to a special well behind the driver's seat. (The spare wheel was on the move again in August 1962, this time finding a home in what was regarded as one of the Pickup's greatest assets, the useful storage locker below the platform.)

Such moves were engineered to allow a full-length flatbed to be created of some 45 square feet. Inevitably, the air-cooling louvres also had to be re-positioned, being cut into the body behind the rear wheel arches. The weatherproof top-hinged locker below the flatbed accounted for a further 20 square feet of space. Hinged side flaps ensured that loads were not only easily accessible, but also unlikely to shoot off into the wild blue yonder when the vehicle accelerated away from whatever site it happened to be working on.

Top, Middle and Bottom Right: *To accompany their brochure artistry (Top Right) Volkswagen described the Pickup as having a 'wide open floor', "16-cubic foot. of loading space under tarpaulin", plus "65-square foot of floor space." Even better, the Pickup had a "total load capacity of 1,764lbs." Thanks to their purpose in life, not as many Pickups have survived. The two examples depicted, Middle and Bottom Right, both date from the mid-1960s, at a point when the front indicators had been enlarged and average yearly production totalled around 38,000 vehicles.*

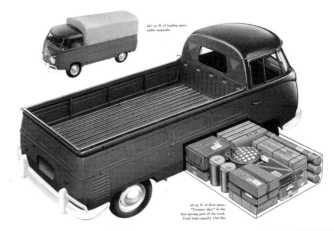

Top Left: *The Pickup, loaned itself to approved special conversions. Here it has been adapted to carry a hydraulic lifting platform – option SO9.*

Middle Left: *"Goods and people: your transport problem, the six-passenger Pickup will solve it. 3-people plus 430 lbs load in rear cabin and 827 lbs load on platform, 6-people plus 827 lbs load on platform".*

Bottom Left: *The Double-Cab Pickup became popular very quickly, and as the brochure pointed out, solved the problem of carrying both goods and more than two people.The German Fire Service made effective use of the vehicle that is pictured here.*

In all, 1,606 Pickups were produced between August 1952 and the end of the year, while by 1959, that total had risen to 24,465 units. Throughout the 1960s in excess of 30,000 pickups were produced each year.

Early advertising text for the Pickup extols the virtues of the vehicle more successfully than any other in the range. From "the clever way in which the most is made of every inch of space indicated how thoughtfully the Volkswagen Pickup was designed" to "the Volkswagen Pickup has what others do not – a lower compartment", its assets were exposed for all to appreciate. By the mid-1960s, the message justifiably was more of the same. "The VW Pickup is absolutely flat: no wheel housing is in the way. It's big: the platform is 8'6" long and 5' 1" wide, giving an area of 45 square feet. Easy to load: Both side and tailboards can be let down. It's robust: Hardwood slats protect the corrugated platform and stop cargo from slipping. It has a large lockable compartment under the platform between the axles which is absolutely dry and which gives you 20 square feet more load space".

In October 1958 the Pickup became available with either a wooden platform or a wide bed, the latter increasing the load size from a 45 to a 55 square foot area and the overall width by some 13 inches. Both were initiated to satisfy the demands made by members of the building trade. During the following month, yet another Pickup variant was launched. This time it was the Double Cab or Crew Cab, a vehicle that again required reasonably extensive re-tooling by its makers. Apart from the need for a larger roof panel, a rear cab side-door had to be fabricated, as had a shorter bed and a revised cab. Gone was that much flaunted dry-weather lower storage area, although there was room for some articles below the new rear bench seat.

The final major addition to the range of Splittie Transporters was the High-Roof, or High Top Delivery Van. Available from September 1961, thanks to VW's model year policy, it was marketed as a 1962 addition. The enlarged roof was made out of steel, at least in VW's eyes an essential ingredient of the package, ensuring rigidity. Taller doors and extended body panels resulted in a model that stood 90" from the ground to the top of the roof, compared to 75½" for the normal Delivery Van. Apart from its popularity with members of the glazing and clothing trade, the High-Roof Delivery Van was eminently suitable for conversion to both a camper or mobile catering unit, thanks to its extra headroom.

The copywriters extolled the virtues of the new addition. "You have still longer, wider or higher objects to transport? Well then, this is the van for you. It's 14" higher than the normal delivery van. The mean height is 66.1". And the load compartment has 212 cubic feet of space. Therefore, you have more room to move in this van and it's easier to get at things. There's really room to swing the proverbial cat. In addition it has even larger doors and an even larger side area for advertising".

For several years after the first Transporter made its debut, Volkswagen publicity included a model that at face value seemed highly inappropriate for 'consumption' by the general public, be they firms or individuals. Launched in December 1951, following a brief period of sub-contracting to the German firm of Miesen, the VW Ambulance remained part of the array throughout the years of the Splittie and beyond. Sales inevitably came nowhere near the rest of the range, with 481 being produced in 1952, rising to the twin peaks of 883 in 1961 and 864 four-years later in 1965. So integral to the original range was the Ambulance that it was designated with its own unique identifying code. If the Type 21 was the Delivery Van and the Kombi was the Type 23, then the Ambulance was known as the Type 27.

Top and Bottom Right: *Unlike its successors, the original incarnation of the High-Top Delivery Van was constructed completely out of steel. Something of a rarity these days, the camping fraternity who preferred home-spun conversions found an ideal 'donor' in the High-Top version of the Panelvan. The vehicle illustrated Top Right has been fitted with American specification bumpers, a somewhat unusual choice for this vehicle, while the Transporter Bottom Right appears to be finished in primer, an option from Volkswagen when house liveries and advertising decals were to be applied.*

It was foreseen from the start that there would be many variations both on and from the official Transporter model listings. A range of special options soon started to materialise, with the 1951 parts manuals listing SP, or Special Set, equipment. By 1960, no less than an astonishing 130 variations on the theme were listed, a selection of which are noted below. A 1964 brochure even went so far as to list a range of suggestions for one-off specials, complete with artists' sketches if the special hadn't been built previously.

Although Volkswagen equipped some of the vehicles, most were palmed out to specialist coachbuilders and it is through such practice that the most popular of all Transporters, the ubiquitous camper, evolved. Conceivably the inclusion of the Ambulance in publicity material was intended to convey the diversity of possible uses. If this was the case, the ploy worked exceptionally well.

By the very nature of its role, the VW Ambulance required an enlarged and opening tailgate, which in turn ruled out the notion of a barn-door engine compartment lid. VW therefore offered the forerunner of all smaller engine lids from the start. Compilers of text for the brochures, denied the convenience of describing in detail aspects of the ambulance that would be of interest only to doctors and nursing staff, were almost lost for words, but not quite! "Every feature has been planned to give patients maximum comfort. Standard equipment for Volkswagen Ambulances includes two stretchers mounted at the same level on each side of the ambulance, an upholstered removable seat for carrying patients up and down narrow stairs, a further well-upholstered seat for patients and a folding-seat for the medical attendant next to the patients. The cabin seats the driver and two stretcher bearers".

Special models included a mobile shop, a vehicle to convey frozen food, a hydraulic tipper truck, an exhibition and display bus, a mobile library and even a hearse. Interestingly, the Westfalia Camper and 'Camper Kit', originally known as a 'Camping Box', were amongst the options. However, VW never produced campers as such themselves.

SPLITTIE DEVELOPMENT

Inevitably, with a production run of 17-years, the original version of the Transporter attracted countless detail changes. At its launch, the Transporter was gifted the Beetle's 25bhp engine, which, considering the extra weight it was asked to cope with, still managed to produce a creditable 25mpg. As the purpose of the Transporter wasn't to travel from point A to B in the fastest possible time, a top speed of 50mph wasn't detrimental, while 0-40mph in 22.7 seconds, was highly competitive.

Initially the Transporter lacked any form of rear window and until November 1950 a prominent VW roundel made it abundantly apparent to a following driver that the vehicle was produced by Volkswagen.

Above: *This pre-March 1955 Kombi perhaps best illustrates why Volkswagen's Transporter hit the motoring world by storm. As with the Beetle and later the VW1500, Volkswagen's policy was to make continual improvements. Ingenious variations on the Transporter theme made it even more successful, and the Kombi was the true forerunner of today's multi-purpose vehicle.*

Less than six-months later, in April 1951, a tiny window was added but rearward access to the interior was still denied. Early models also lacked a rear bumper, with Deluxe models gaining this 'luxury' from March 1953 and more lowly offerings, following suite in December. The Pickup had a further wait, with a rear bumper arriving in April 1954.

Eavesdrop on the conversation of an enthusiast and the term 'barn door' could well enter any discussion. The term refers to the extraordinarily large, top-hinged engine lid of the early days, a feature that dwarfed the contents, consisting of a vertically mounted spare wheel, plus a precariously and potentially lethally mounted fuel tank and filler almost directly above the 25bhp engine. While the spare wheel soon adopted a horizontal position on the equivalent of a tray, partially dividing the fuel filler from direct contact with the engine, it was 1955 before fuel could be put into the vehicle externally. The tank was relocated to a position near the back axle at the same time, while the barn door became a thing of the past.

Until March 1953, the Transporter sported a crash box. From October 1952, synchromesh on second, third and fourth gears, made driving the Transporter child's play. First gear finally acquired synchromesh in May 1959, thanks to the introduction of a wholly revised gearbox. The Splittie was always fitted with reduction boxes, which utilised a totally separate oil supply, and were located on the end of the axle tubes.

December 1953, witnessed the first upgrading of the Transporter's engine, from 25bhp to 30bhp. Increasing the bore from 75mm to 77mm, and the compression ratio from 5.8:1 to 6.1:1, (and to 6.6:1 in August 1954) enlarged the capacity to 1192cc. The 30bhp unit was redesigned in May 1959, with a detachable dynamo pedestal being the most noticeable visual difference. The new engine was quieter, thanks to the reduced speed of the cooling fan, but it was only in June 1960, when the power was increased to 34bhp, that the difference was noticeable.

Below: *The panoramic rear window had arrived in August 1963, while the engine lid concealed a useful 1500cc powerhouse, the less well-endowed 1200cc engine finally being dropped from the range in October 1965.*

With effect from January 1963, Volkswagen offered Transporter owners the option of the engine fitted to the relatively recently introduced VW 1500 saloon and variant. Initially restricted to vehicles sold in the USA, from March of the same year the 1493cc, 42bhp engine was also available to all other markets, although it was only an option on vehicles of Kombi specification or above. With the advent of the new model year in August, even the lowly Panel van and Pickup could be specified with the more powerful engine. By October 1965, part way through the 1966 model year, the demand for the 1200 engine was negligible and it was quietly deleted as an option. A direct result of the introduction of the 1500 power unit was an increase in the Transporter's payload from 750kg to 1,000kg, while the vehicle's top speed was boosted to 65mph. From August 1964, ever cautious and conservative Volkswagen fitted a governor to ensure that owners didn't break the rules! Three-months earlier, larger valves had been fitted, resulting in improved engine breathing, while increasing brake horsepower to 44.

The earliest Transporters operated with a speedometer that appeared to run backwards, but this was 'corrected' in March 1953. Far more extensive improvements occurred exactly two-years later. The most noticeable change was a totally redesigned peaked roof, creating a frontal overhang, ideal for the insertion of intakes for cab ventilation. A close second was the abolition of the 'barn door' and in its place the arrival of both a smaller engine lid and a useful opening tailgate. Perhaps the reduction of wheel sizes, from 16 to 15 inches wasn't instantly apparent. However, the introduction of an admittedly rather basic full length dash on all models, replacing the single instrument binnacle, previously the hallmark of all options except the Microbus Deluxe, couldn't be missed.

Volkswagen was the main manufacturer that clung onto the increasingly antiquated semaphore indicators longer than most. However, for models bound for the USA and Canada, 'modern' flashers became the norm in April 1955. Over five-years later, in June 1960, Europe caught up but, at the end of July 1961, American exports leapt ahead once more with the arrival of another feature which has gained its own enthusiast terminology. Larger and flatter, the new front indicators were soon named 'fish-eyes'. In August 1963, other markets were allowed to catch up! Also initially a US exclusive, from August 1958, all Transporters were fitted with a revised style of two-tier bumper, which soon became popular as an accessory elsewhere.

In May 1963, a sliding door became an extra cost option, but to the end of Splittie production it never developed into a standard part of the Transporter's package. Three-months later, in August 1963, the rear window was increased in size, sadly deleting the two wraparound rear windows on the Microbus Deluxe as a result. August 1965, saw another quirky feature vanish, as the so-called 'church key', which had previously been used to open the engine lid, was replaced with a conventional push-button. Finally, in 1966, candle-like six-volt electric's became a thing of the past, with the arrival of floodlighting and 12-volts.

Although incidental to the catalogue of changes listed above, in March 1956 a brand new factory, which had taken just a year to build, became the Transporter's home. The decision to relocate to Hanover hadn't been determined by a lack of available capacity, but was the result of Wolfsburg's limited pool of workers from which to draw on.

Top, Middle and Bottom Right: *After semaphores came 'bullet' style front indicators (Top Right). These in turn were replaced by 'fish-eye' indicators (Middle Right). Meanwhile, (Bottom Right) the number of cooling vents increased over the years and changed from outward to inward facing. From 1955 until 1966, the petrol filler door was opened with a 'church key'.*

SPLITTIE FACTS AND FIGURES

Although various facts and figures have been banded about already, it's worth summarising General Director Nordhoff's achievements with the 17-year run of his commercial vehicle. In all 1,833,000 Transporters were built between 1950, (or 1949 when the prototypes are taken into consideration), and the end of July 1967. Between 1958 and 1961, an additional 52,900 completely knocked down (CKD) kits were 'built' at Hanover, destined for assembly at VW's satellites. The South African and Australian operations were responsible for the manufacture of an additional 35,000 Splitties before 1968, while in Brazil Splittie production continued until 1975, accounting for close on 400,000 more Transporters.

In 1954, when both Transporter and Beetle production had got into full swing and before other models joined Volkswagen's range, the Transporter accounted for close on 17% of the company's total volume. In 1966, the last full year of Splittie manufacture, the combined production run of Beetles and Transporters totalled 1,271,538 vehicles, of which the commercial vehicle accounted for 15%.

Above: *Every option was depicted on the cover of this late first generation brochure entitled: "What's the VW Commercial got to write home about?" Note the Pickup with wide platform and the Ambulance directly behind it.*

In 1964, after switching Transporter production from Wolfsburg to the purpose-built Hanover plant in 1956; another new factory started producing Transporters exclusively for export. This was the Emden factory, which also churned out Beetles as fast as countries like the USA and Canada demanded them.

Exports were always important to VW's success story and, while many know that by the 1960s, Volkswagen were proudly proclaiming that their Beetle was a favourite in a total of 136 countries around the world, the Transporter became an equally accomplished globetrotter. As far back as 1950, countries like Brazil, Belgium, the Netherlands, Sweden and Switzerland, to name some of the main export destinations, were familiar with the Splittie. In Britain, from a solitary example in 1953, the best year for sales was 1964, with 3,800 finding their way across the channel.

Above: *This Microbus Deluxe, or Samba, dates from 1952 to early 1955. It is painted in Chestnut Brown over Sealing Wax Red. That it is a Deluxe model can be determined by the additional bright-work running along the waistline of the van's side, the 'V' on its front and even on the metalwork between its wheels. The prominent VW symbol is chromed, as are the hubcaps. Additional windows in the form of skylights and the scarcely noticeable fold-back sunroof are further giveaways. One look at the interior would have been sufficient to confirm the vehicle's chart-topping status even to the rawest of recruits in Transporter appreciation.*

Right: *Throughout the 1950s, Volkswagen relied on the skills of Bernd Reuters to promote its Transporter. The artist was clever, for not only did he streamline and elongate his subject, but also tended to reduce the scale of the vehicle's occupants.*

25

Above: *Without doubt one of the reasons for the success of the Transporter was the ability to adapt the basic body-shape to a whole host of uses. At the dawn of the 1960s VW proudly listed 130 variations, although as early as 1951 the first references to 'specials' had been made. Amongst the more interesting, practical, or simply bizarre, were a High Roof Mobile Shop, an Exhibition and Display Bus, a Catastrophe and Disaster Emergency Vehicle, a Snow Plough and a Catering Van. The example of this last mentioned 'conversion' depicted, dates from the mid-1960s.*

Left: *Transporters used as fire-trucks had their own model code by 1952, while, as in this instance, other operations adapted VW's product to their own specification. Most Panelvan 'conversions' carried three fire fighters, suitable equipment and a VW Industrial Engine water pump.*

Above: *The second generation Transporter easily outsold its predecessor in a considerably shorter period of time. For example nearly 51,000 Panelvans were produced in its first full year of production, a figure never achieved previously. However, unlike its predecessor, the vehicle peaked in the mid-1970s when it still had several years more to run. This particular van is a later model (April 1978), and is identifiable by front indicators positioned above, rather than below the headlamps, plus a smaller VW roundel on its front. It is finished in Neptune Blue.*

Right: *Although two-tone paint schemes were only standard on the luxury version of the Microbus, many seen on the roads today exhibit this feature. This is because they have been converted to camper vans, another reason why the Kombi and Microbus, (the ideal host for such adaptations), sold so well. As a finishing touch the converter invariably offered a two-tone paint scheme.*

Above: *At first glance this third generation Transporter looks like any other of its ilk. However, if the decals down its side weren't a complete giveaway, its high off-the-ground stance should be. For this is a 'Syncro' model, as developed by Steyr-Daimler-Puch in Austria. It had permanent all-wheel drive via a viscous clutch, while Volkswagen produced the body and engine as normal. By March 1989, 25,000 such vehicles had been built. Although a new model replaced the third generation Transporter in 1990, production of the Syncro continued until September 1992.*

Left: *Camper conversion specialists found the third generation Transporter ideal, thanks to its spacious interior. This example is an early model, identifiable by its lack of a second grille on the front, a hallmark of its water-cooled successor. Note also, how the headlamp arrangements changed during the vehicle's lifetime.*

TRADITIONALLY MODERN – THE BAY

Whereas the first generation Transporter revelled in a period of continual expansion, sound investments and healthy profits, under the umbrella of a single Director General, the new model, launched in August 1967, would fare incredibly differently. Although very much planned and conceived under the old regime (for the process had started in 1964), within less than a year of its arrival, there was a new man at the top, who had a very different agenda to that of Heinz Nordhoff. To complicate issues further, Germany and the rest of Europe had just been through the first real recession since the war, which somehow created a changed atmosphere over the next few years, when crises in the form of oil shortages and roaring inflation would rock the automobile industry, amongst others, to its very core.

The second incarnation of the Transporter was produced for a little under 12-years, during which time VW had four Director Generals. Heinz Nordhoff died in April 1968. Kurt Lotz was ousted in the autumn of 1971, having set in motion the first airy-fairy and disastrous steps to rid VW of its air-cooled legacy. Rudolf Leiding's reign was equally short, when in February 1975 Toni Schmücker became Director General.

Above: *This picture shows the basic Transporter range as presented on the introduction of the new range in August 1967. Back-row: Panelvan and Kombi. Middle-row: Clipper (Deluxe) and Clipper. Front-row: Double and single cab Pickup.* Volkswagen press photo

Leiding was the man who, having decided that he could not turn VW's clock back by four years, put in place a realistic strategy to produce the Passat, Golf and Polo, but at a terrible sales and financial cost to Volkswagen. Schmücker inevitably received a great deal of the credit for Leiding's actions. He axed the Beetle from German production, the rest of Nordhoff's air-cooled family already having gone. The sole exception however, was the Transporter, which, to be brutally honest, remained the mainstay of any gleam of profitability during this troubled period.

In the year of Nordhoff's death, Volkswagen turned in a healthy profit of 339-million DM. By 1971, this had fallen to a mere12-million DM. Leiding appeared to turn things around a little, his best year being 1973, when 109-million DM was achieved. However, 1974 saw a 555-million DM loss, partly due to the oil crisis, which VW could do little about.

The main reason for Volkswagen's heavy losses in 1974, however, was the record level of investments, which stood at 1,187-million DM, the monies being used to get the new water-cooled range up and running. With the Golf and its companions in place and successful (except in the USA, which is a story in itself), Volkswagen bedded down into a pattern of healthy profits and sound investment.

In April 1975, Volkswagen launched a new larger water-cooled commercial vehicle, with both petrol and diesel engine options. Named the LT, it was soon available in a wide variety of guises, including a straightforward Panelvan, plus a high roof option, a versatile Pickup, embracing an optional low load platform, or simply a chassis plus driver's cab. The LT was available in three weight categories, ranging from 2.8, via 3.1, to 3.5 tons. The LT's rugged capabilities were enhanced by good performance, a reputation earned largely on the back of the Audi 100 derived petrol engine.

Above: *Although VW had a brand new model to boast about, the brochure copywriters were content to write that the Transporter had "been given a facelift".* VW Brochure

Although some might interpret the arrival of the LT as direct competition to the older air-cooled model, Transporter sales remained reasonably buoyant. From the 253,919 produced in the first full year of production, numbers hovered at a little under the 300,000 mark, only experiencing a serious fall in the disastrous year of 1974, when (from the 289,022 Transporters built in 1973) the figure dropped to 222,233. From here it witnessed a slight revival in 1976 to 234,912 units, but gradually tailed away. The Bay was the representative of the breed that witnessed the passing of the two-million barrier in 1968, the third in September 1971 and the fourth in July 1975. By the time the model bowed out, 4.8 million Transporters had been built since 1950, of which the Bay accounted for three million!

Unlike the first generation of Transporters, of which staged introductions had taken over 11-years to complete (if the high top version of the Panel Van is included), the new model had to be available in its various options from the word go. All the major choices from the earlier version survived, including, for example, the Pickup with an extended platform, the Double Cab and even the Ambulance. Almost all retained their names as well, except the most amended Transporter of all, the range topping Microbus Deluxe, which became the Clipper. Sadly, although the new Transporter exhibited many advantages, in Clipper form some of its most endearing features, like the skylight windows, fold-back cloth sunroof and heavy use of additional bright work were lost forever.

As it turned out, the new name for the range topper wasn't destined to be long lived. Not that the model with a steel crank-operated sunroof, additional mouldings on the bumper and a little supplementary shiny metal adorning its front in the form of the VW roundel, and sides, in the shape of chromed hubcaps and window inserts, didn't sell. The problem was that the British Overseas Airways Corporation (BOAC), had been running a Clipper Class service to the USA for some years and objected to VW pilfering the name for its van.

After a short but acrimonious row, Volkswagen conceded defeat and from then on the Microbus was available in two versions: plain and simple and the 'L' model, a term entirely in keeping with policy across the rest of the Volkswagen family, but lacking the character of their first choice.

The only serious contender to be late for the launch was the high-top version of the Panel Van, which eventually made its debut in January 1968. However, with its arrival, and to the horror of the traditionalist, Volkswagen had abandoned the principle of an all-steel vehicle, preferring instead to produce a kit-car style roof for the High Top, made out of fibreglass. Although recognition had come that, with an all-steel high roof, performance suffered, somehow fibreglass just wasn't VW. What however, the use of such material did do was to send a signal to all the companies converting Transporters to caravans, to explore similar avenues.

Below: *"The VW Clipper Estate Car … A finger light, though robust and close fitting sliding door, easy access plus full family car comfort for the driver make this the ideal teenage family car …"*
Press and Public Relations Department, Volkswagen GB.

Wolfsburg's design team were entirely convincing in their aim of creating much more than a revised version of the Transporter. Apart from the hidden technical advances, visually the looks of the second generation were altogether different than those of the first. Although perhaps not quite so happy and smiling a look prevailed, nevertheless the stance was both modern and appealing, without resorting to the gimmicks employed by some manufacturers.

Both the wheelbase and the width of the new vehicle were similar to that of the older model, but a 160mm increase in its length, thanks to an extra 100mm overhang at both ends of the Transporter, made it look bigger. Although construction was similarly unitary in nature to that of the Splittie, the new model was sturdier and benefited from a larger interior space. This was created partly due to the aforementioned increase in length, but also thanks to a lower floor, although the overall height of the vehicle was not affected. The Splittie stood 1925mm from the ground; the new model just 15mm higher at 1940mm. That a lower floor was possible was due to a new double joint rear axle with semi trailing links.

At the same time the reduction boxes associated with the Splittie were consigned to the archives, while up front king and link pins were replaced with maintenance-free ball joints.

Above: *If any model suffered a loss of identity when the Bay Transporter made its debut, it was the Microbus Deluxe. Although extra trim can be seen, together with a half-hearted attempt at two-tone paint and extras attached to the bumpers, its lack of extra windows etc, made it more or less indistinguishable from the rest.*
Press and Public Relations Department Volkswagen GB

Without itemising every detail, save to mention that the track was increased by 625mm and a front anti-roll bar was fitted, we might summarise and say that the new set up ensured both better road holding and handling.

Powering the Transporter was the VW 1600 family car's 1584cc engine (see the Nostalgia Road book *Volkswagen Cars 1948-1968* by the same author). Offering 47bhp at 4000rpm, although by no means the fastest commercial vehicle on the road, it was an improvement on the Splittie and had the advantage over its rivals both in terms of longevity and the ability to cruise all day at 65mph. Acceleration times through the gears remained more or less as before, but then the new model had put on a little weight. Although drum brakes were still the order of the day at both front and rear, dual circuit brakes ensured less chance of fatalities in the case of partial failure.

Visually, it was the change to the front windscreen that did most to modernise the Transporter's looks. Now 27% larger and being panoramic with wraparound edges, the screen's appearance quickly led to the new vehicle being dubbed the Bay. The front panel was also flatter. Rectangular indicators positioned close to a modern, sturdier, squarer bumper and above all, the distinctive 'state of the art' fresh air grille, made the vehicle appear bang up to date and dramatically much more modern.

Instead of the four or five square side windows on the Splittie people-carrying Transporters, the Bay featured larger, sleeker, rectangular ones. So large were they that there was little room down the side of the vehicle for anything else, other than the air intake louvres required to duct cool air to the engine. The cab doors were 625mm wider on the Bay than they had been previously, while the windows cranked rather then slid. However, the best improvement of all in practical terms was the replacement of the two narrow, pull open side doors with a single sliding one. Larger mirrors and cunningly concealed door hinges, more or less completed the main improvements to the new model's external appearance.

Internally, much of the austerity of the Splittie was banished. Most notable was the new dash, a thoroughly modern affair largely moulded and covered in non-reflective vinyl. Although still not over endowed with dials and switches, what there was had been finished in black and made from softer, flat-topped, plastic. A plastic headlining was fitted in the cab of the workaday models and throughout for the people-carrying models, while the seat back-rests and squabs, which were covered in 'breathable' hound-dog tooth vinyl, were larger, shaped and more comfortable.

Below: *This publicity shot depicts the Station Wagon. which VW produced for the North American market.*

Left: *Both the Bays photographed on this page have been converted to campers, although in the case of the bottom vehicle this is not immediately apparent. The Devon Eurovette (Top) dates from 1969 and was based on the Microbus. The Danbury model (Bottom), was a conversion on the more lowly Kombi. Although this particular vehicle wasn't registered until the Autumn of 1972, VW had built the vehicle before the end of July. Visually this is evident thanks to the location of the front indicators, the large size of the VW Roundel and the 'Rounded' Bumpers.*

Volkswagen's copywriters exploited the assets of the new Transporter to the full in a massive wave of literature published to coincide with the vehicle's launch. "The new VW Commercial has had a face-lift. Its looks have been improved. But that's not all. With its new body, it is larger, more elegant. But at the same time much more practical too. The full-width, curved windscreen and (in the Kombi and Clipper) the large side windows mean good visibility and plenty of light inside. The two speed windscreen wipers have large blades. Generous exterior mirrors project on each side giving a really wide rear view.... The flashing indicators up front are new. But this isn't just for art's sake. They're larger too. Which makes them even easier to see than before. The sturdy wraparound bumpers are just the right height above the ground – and the front incorporates a step on either side. No more clambering into the cab. The new VW Commercial is a distinctive, elegant vehicle. And a fast one. Like it?"

To promote the Transporter range, the bold headlines tumbled out, thick and fast: "The new VW Commercial has a spacious cab with passenger comfort to make your workaday life more comfortable … has a new instrument panel to give you fingertip control … has a new effective heating and ventilation system to ensure you're never too hot or too cold … even has a large sliding door as a standard fitting to make it easier to load and unload … has separate seats in the cab to provide direct access to the load compartment … has passenger car characteristics to give a smoother ride".

The range was described thus: Delivery Van "with a 2205lb payload", Kombi "with 177 cu ft of load space or seating for seven or eight", plus a "Pick-Up with flat load surface and as VW Double Cab Pick-Up with 31.2 sq ft of load surface and six seats". For the range-topping Microbuses, the "VW Clipper – with passenger car comfort and more than ample space for passengers and luggage as VW Clipper L – with even greater comfort".

Press reaction to the new Transporter was extremely positive. Typical of the brownie points brigade was the report in *Popular Imported Cars*, which was published in March 1968 and proclaimed: "Long modern appearance ...excellent driver visibility ... the inside of the vehicle now has what can be called décor. ... Thorough planning went into the integration of the new vinyl upholstery and the padding to produce a beautiful modern interior ... The final result of ... suspension changes is passenger car like ride and handling that has to be tried to be believed ... All in all the VW 'boxes' have been considerably improved in all the important areas".

If there were any signs of criticism, they came when performance was discussed. One of the harshest was *World Car Guide*, who in their March 1970 issue went to town on the lack of oomph with the Bay. Their reporter found "it will accelerate from zero to 60mph in 37.11 seconds", while "... the gas pedal must be floored most of the time, unless you want to stay in the truck lane" A parting swipe at the engine's meagre output came with the plea to "remember to drive defensively, as there is no power whatever in reserve to bail you out of an error in judgement at today's highway speeds ..."

Although Volkswagen crumbled and tottered after Nordhoff's death, at least the Bay wasn't neglected, being upgraded both performance wise and in its appearance. In many ways the old and sound policy of continual improvement was still in play, although inevitably the new VW bosses must have been influenced by any adverse press comments made about models in the range.

The first engine upgrade came in 1970, for the '71 model year, when the 1600 engine was modified with twin-port cylinder heads. Apart from more efficient running and better 'breathing', the effect was to increase the unit's power output to 50bhp. There was no attempt to mate the engine to twin carburettors, or even to upgrade the barrels and pistons, so although long-term enthusiasts were greatly impressed, some journalists weren't convinced.

Top, Middle and Bottom Right: *Although body modifications were relatively few, VW upgraded the engine on several occasions during the second generation Transporter. The Westfalia camper conversion shown Top Right (with its roof elevated) dates from 1976. This vehicle was powered by the faithful, if slothful, twin-port, 1600 engine which is seen close-up in the Middle Right illustration; however, by this time a two-litre power unit was also on offer. The dash, Bottom Right, changed little.*

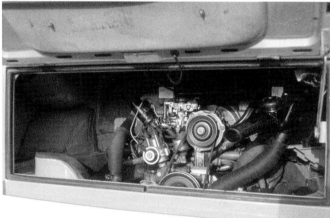

Volkswagen responded, by adopting the engine from the VW 411, the largest member of the air-cooled family, as an option on all Transporters other than the Pickup. (In the USA it became standard across the entire range)

The 'new' engine gave a very useful boost to the Bay in the performance stakes. With a capacity of 1679cc, the 1.7 litre flat four produced 66bhp at 4,800rpm. With a pair of useful Solex 34 carburettors, the vehicle was capable of what in Transporter terms, was an earth-shattering top speed of 76mph, while 0-60 times became much more acceptable at 22 seconds.

Having adopted the large family car's engine once, VW did it all over again, in August 1973 for the '74 year model with a 1795cc, 1.8-litre engine. Although the top speed only increased by 4mph and bhp rose by just two, while fuel consumption

Above: *Improved safety was the main feature of the 1973 VW Pickup, which was distinguishable from its predecessors by its raised front indicators and redesigned bumpers.*
Volkswagen Press Photo

dropped down to a thirsty 20mpg, the further increase in power meant that the Transporter could definitely keep up with the rest of the pack. In the USA Bosch fuel injection became standard.

From August 1975, the largest ever air-cooled engine found its way into the Transporter as a companion to the more lowly 1600, which still soldiered on in most markets. As the VW 412, the successor to the 411, was already a thing of the past, the beefy two-litre engine was borrowed from the joint project VW-Porsche 914.

Rumours of a 2.2-litre air-cooled engine never materialised for the Bay, presumably because in a water-cooled world, there was nothing available to borrow and the development of an engine for one model was deemed inappropriate. The reality of the two-litre engine was that it was the 1800 with an increased bore and stroke, realising 70bhp at 4,200rpm in the process. Twin carbs remained the order of the day for most markets, while the USA continued to favour fuel-injection. Although VW regarded 80mph as a maximum, once the 1970cc lump had loosened up, many found it capable of the proverbial 'ton'. Whatever else, torque was up by some eight per cent, which once again assisted hill climbing, resulting in a vehicle that was rarely left on the starting line.

Press reaction to the two-litre wasn't entirely devoid of adverse comments, but was sufficiently positive for comparative tests to keep the Volkswagen at the head of the list. Britain's *Safer Motoring Volkswagen* magazine wrote, "It will out accelerate many cars and easily cruise at the legal limit on the motorways, regardless of headwinds or hills". *Auto, Motor and Sport* cheered the "very rapid acceleration in traffic", while *Car South Africa* praised the gain in torque, noting it was "immediately apparent when driving, particularly when it [came] to climbs". However, they were quick to add that "even with 2-litres and a good spread of torque" the Transporter was "no performance vehicle", but "acceleration in the gears" was "greatly enhanced in the new model and gradient ability show[ed] a marked improvement as well".

If an inordinate amount of space appears to have been bestowed on the guts of the Bay, then it only demonstrates that Volkswagen had never chopped and changed so much before.

Below: *According to VW's publicity machine; "This Microbus is a large passenger car. And it drives like one too. Available with automatic transmission, which makes it the complete passenger car".*
Volkswagen Press Photo, 1973

When it came to bodywork updates and additional models with the Bay, they were more or less in step with those involving the model's predecessor. Here are the ones that caught the headlines, itemised in some sort of chronological order.

In August 1970, the van finally acquired disc brakes. The wheel design was altered too, with the introduction of circular holes designed to aid cooling and disperse heat. Although the size of the wheels neither increased nor decreased, they did become wider. The anachronism of domed hubcaps, dispensed with on the Beetle in the mid-1960s finally ended with the arrival of the less attractive, flat variety.

The following year the engine cooling louvres located behind the side windows were increased in size to suit the heftier 1700 engine. The tail-lights became larger too.

A post-August 1973 model is easy to identify, thanks to the re-positioning of the front indicator lamps from a bumper hugging low location, to a position above the headlamps.

Above: *This Volkswagen press photo, dating from 1973, depicts the re-vamped version of the top of the range Microbus L. Re-positioned front indicators and sturdier 'U-shaped' bumpers were the hallmarks of this revised model.*

Additionally the size of the front panel mounted VW symbol was reduced, becoming less heavy-looking. Stronger, crumple-absorbing bumpers were fitted at both front and rear. The step to assist clambering into the cab (located at the end of the older style front bumper) disappeared, while the Microbus was available with an extra cost option of a chromed front bumper. Of more importance was the arrival of a crumple zone in the cab floor. Primarily for the US market, the 1700 version of the Transporter became available as a three-speed automatic. The press reaction was interesting. *PV4* wrote that, "there seems to be little loss of power through the box. The shift is positive and snappy …".

Top Right: *Although at first glance this Brazilian-built Transporter appears similar to European-built models, the reader should note the combination of older style bumpers against indicators above the headlamps, plus (crucially) the multiplicity of side and rear windows. A Kombi model, it dates from 1982.*

Middle Right: *This 1982 Brazilian built Pickup sports a diesel engine, hence the add-on radiator at the front.*

Bottom Right: *This 2004 Brazilian-built model could be bought in this country ready converted into a camper.*

By the mid-1970s, the humble old bus was being described by some as an in-vogue alternative to the numerous more up-market and larger family saloons available from rival manufacturers. Tinted windows, an extra cost option on both the Kombi and the Microbus, plus a retracting step and a heated rear screen on the latter, were enough to make some stop and think.

In the Bay's final years, luxury became the main talking (if not selling) point, although in 1978 five prototype four-wheel-drive vehicles were produced. Sadly, perhaps due to the success VW were experiencing with their water-cooled cars, the four-wheel option disappeared in a tide of management apathy. As a consequence, Volkswagen missed the boat in what could have been an ideal means of generating extra Transporter sales.

In 1978, the Microbus could be bought garnished with metallic silver paint and the plushest of velour upholstery. Price was definitely an issue. No longer was the Transporter simply a 'box on wheels' for the man in the street. Whether it was $10,000 with all the trimmings in the USA, 9,000 Rand in South Africa for the all-singing, all-dancing automatic, or 20,000 DM in Germany with the extras thrown in, VW had moved the goalposts, believing there to be more disposable income available in the majority of countries. Fair comment, no doubt, but this policy, which was carried forward into the next generation, was one of the main reasons that others began to aspire to the Transporter's crown.

Although the Bay ebbed its last in 1979 as far as German production was concerned, just like the Beetle before it, production continued in South America. In Mexico it finally came to a halt in 1998, but the results of Brazilian manufacture were readily available via the 'grey market' when this book was written. Inevitably, the Bay developed, one of the oddest changes (thankfully not all encompassing), being the addition of an ugly radiator at its front to accommodate water-cooling!

THE THIRD GENERATION, DIVERSITY AND COMPLEXITY

Toni Schmücker, Director General number four in VW's post-war history, had been in the driving seat for considerably less than six months, when he made a decision that would astound many would-be Transporter purchasers when it became reality. Nobody knows whether it was a lack of experience, knowledge that VW's water-cooled range, although launched, hadn't as yet bounced into full action, or a reluctance to spend development money at a time when VW was up to its ears in accumulated debts, which determined Schmücker to decree in May 1975 that the third generation Transporter would have an air-cooled, rear-mounted engine. However, he is on record as stating that competition to the concept of a box on wheels was non-existent, thanks to its 'particular design and mechanics'. The design department at VW, working with Gustav Mayer, weren't impressed, being keenest to break the mould and drop in a water-pumper up-front! Thanks to careful assimilation of customer requests made by the designers, Volkswagen's new Transporter, launched after production began in May 1979, was an instant success.

Above: *When launched, the third generation Transporter models, officially designated the Type 25, were available with either a 1600 or two-litre air-cooled engine. The Volkswagen press photo of the T25 Pickup clearly shows one grille with headlights at either end. Later models with water-cooled engines had a second grille below the first grille and above the box-section bumpers.*

Of course the marketing men, PR barons and copywriting gurus, faced a collective ribbing as they struggled to come to terms with promoting a flat four air-cooled engine, when for half a decade they had been politely ditching the Beetle.

The new Transporter was altogether different from its immediate predecessor. For a start it was bigger, and in appearance the T25 bore more than a passing resemblance to its big brothers in the LT range, lacking the distinctively smiley features of both the Bay and Splittie. With as much aesthetic charm as a brick, perhaps it wasn't a surprise that its nickname soon became 'The Wedge'. For a period after the third generation Transporter's demise, Wedges hit rock bottom prices. Then suddenly, as Bays became expensive, the interest revived!

40

Nowadays a Wedge is as sound an investment as a gold ingot, with values rising in some instances by more than 40% year on year. While Splitties might have reached silly prices and some Bays fetch 'second mortgage' sums, inevitably there is a knock-on effect with the third generation Transporter..

Allegedly, producing a large box that went some way to being sympathetic to aerodynamics was the design team's aim. Indeed, their resulting creation did encourage higher top speeds out of the air-cooled lump and less of a hole in wallets at the petrol pumps. Up front, the design assumed more of a curve, while the area above the air-intake grille was raked at the steepest of angles.

Bigger windows predominated, with the front screen increasing in size by 21%, while at the rear the glassed area grew by an extravagant 98%. Round headlamps and retention of a much smaller VW roundel, helped to demonstrate that this was still a product from the VW mould. The slab-like nature of the T25's sides, really broken only by a waist-level swage line, was accentuated by a virtually flat roof, which, while allowing more headroom for passengers, hadn't the rounded comfortable feeling of the Bay.

On a distinctly retrograde note, access to the engine was via a removable panel within the luggage compartment. While this negated the need for a separate external engine lid, the reality was that the new, enormous rear tailgate turned the tables full circle to barn door Splittie technology. The cab doors were much longer, giving opportunities to scrape chunks of paint off a neighbouring vehicle parked moderately close, while the passenger/storage area sliding door assumed welcoming patio-style proportions. Thanks to a determined effort to save space once occupied by the engine, the luggage platform was lowered by a useful 142.5mm. As draftsmen's pens succumbed to the might of the machine, the computer-designed floor-pan allowed a 100mm lower entry point and albeit invisibly, did away with the old cross members. The result was a lower centre of gravity and a decrease in weight, which meant that heavier loads could be bundled into the Panelvan, as permissible loading weights increased to close on one metric-tonne.

Below: "*The Volkswagen 8-seater Microbus is based on the world's most successful commercial vehicle*", *proclaimed VW's press office*. Volkswagen Press Photo

Most impressive was the enlargement in width, which stood at a bulging 125mm increase, allowing three-people to sit in the front with much greater comfort and an important selling point in a number of markets. In length, VW upped the odds by the even greater amount of 150mm, topping the vehicle off with black-capped plain, girder style bumpers. Thanks to the flat roof, the 10mm increase in overall height seemed far greater.

Increases in track size made the new Transporter more stable. At the front the leap forward was from 1,395mm to 1,570mm and at the rear, a slightly gentler surge prevailed, up from 1,455mm to 1,570mm. Beefy 185 x 14 radial tyres were fitted as standard. Sadly, VW's hallmark torsion bars were costly to manufacture and bulky in the space they occupied. As a result the new front suspension was by upper wishbones, progressive coil springs, with inner telescopic shock absorbers and an anti-roll bar. At the back, suspension was by trailing arms, telescopic dampers and coil springs, which was certainly less radical in its changes. Nowadays, nobody would blink an eye at this kind of set-up, but in 1979, this was simply not the accepted way with a Transporter.

Above: *The Double-cab Pickup proved exceptionally popular, thanks to its ability to carry a good number of passengers, as well as transport bulky loads in its easily accessible loading area. This was an especially useful feature for small tradesmen, like builders, or others who needed to carry both a squad of men and their materials to a site. Note the other two generations of Transporter in the background.*

How VW managed to get away with this and a rehashed, suitcase style, 1.6-litre engine, complete with both hydraulic tappets (that took 10-minutes to run quietly) and a 'pestiferous' umpteen-piece exhaust, when they presented it to traditionalists defies belief. Perhaps it was the hand-me-down disc brakes and the old 2-litre lump that saved the day!

Before looking at model options, it's worth delving into the interior, for here the stylists had given the vehicle the full contemporary look. As a plus, it was easy to imagine that you were sat behind the wheel of a Passat or Golf of similar vintage, but black marks were in order as the timeless qualities of both the Bay and particularly the Splittie, were lost forever.

The third generation Transporter's dashboard was made almost entirely out of plastic. The binnacle shrouded a veritable feast of gauges and rocker-type switches compared to those employed by Volkswagen in previous years. The glovebox was large, while the steering wheel, though lacking flair, looked less like that from a lorry.

Most people thought that the seats were improved, with a greater degree of lateral support and where vinyl was the option rather than cloth; the material design was relatively smooth making cleaning easier. Although the off-white headlining was a full-length affair for most models, only the top of the range Microbus benefited from covered window pillars. The rest had to make do with painted metal. When it came to floor coverings all models except the Microbus were decked out with hard-wearing rubber. The posh model luxuriated in equally serviceable carpeting. Heating came via exchangers in the traditional air-cooled way. Ventilation was improved, with large openings on either side of the dashboard and 'boosters' in the rear passenger compartment.

In general terms the Wedge included stipulatory crumple zones, plus a collapsible steering column, both of which had been features of the Bay. It also won praise for the strength of its body-shell against the offerings of rival manufacturers. Whereas the first water-cooled models of cars from VW's stable featured little in the way of safeguards against corrosion, the Wedge was generously daubed with a rubberised protection on all its seams, while the injection of wax into the body cavities helped to ensure longevity.

Below: *The T25 disaster support vehicle.*

All the options offered with the Bay were carried forward to the third generation models. The top of the range was the Microbus and, while it was unquestionably luxurious when compared to the rest, somehow the model specification didn't work. The manufacturing trend of that time had become one of clean, almost austere lines.

Typical of the period in which it was launched, a minimum of bright-work and a proliferation in the use of plastic was the fashion. Hence, the alloy trim mouldings set into all the window rubbers, tapped onto the slab sides, entwining the fresh air intake grille and balanced on the outside of the windscreen pillars, made the Microbus look something like a gypsy's caravan. That the bumpers had brushed aluminium strips attached above and below a central black area probably wasn't a bad thing. Without a doubt in its basic form, as already mentioned, the bumper was in aesthetic terms, fairly obnoxious! A wash and wipe provision on the rear window and extra sound-proofing in both the doors and the new barn-door tailgate, could only be regarded as genuinely advantageous.

This then was the new Transporter and while during its life span of 11-years as the mainstay of commercial and multi-passenger-carrying it underwent many changes, both in terms of engines and body types, it's perhaps worth looking at production figures to see how it held its head up against its predecessor.

In its first full year of 1980, 217,876 Transporters were produced, but this dropped back to a little over 187,000 the following year. By 1983, the vehicle had taken a further plunge to 155,500 units and this is where it remained until 1986, when VW managed to turn out 161,712 vehicles. Sadly, the revival appears to have been a one-year wonder, as in 1987 just 145,380 Transporters left the factory. Although there was a marginal increase in the next year or two, the lofty heights of the earliest years of Transporter sales were never again achieved. During the 1980s, Volkswagen recorded both magnificent profits and horrendous losses.

Below: *A straightforward water-cooled third generation Panelvan dating from the 1988 model year.*

With effect from January 1982, the VW Empire was under the control of Carl H Hahn, one-time former Nordhoff protégé and VW boss in America. Hahn's stage was far greater than the simple box on wheels as he endeavoured to pull not only Volkswagen, but also its 'subsidiaries', into a global manufacturing operation. As for the Transporter, the simple truth was that after many years ahead in the game, others (most notably the Japanese) had caught up and at very competitive prices.

Although sections of the motoring press expressed surprise at Volkswagen's choice of engine and its location, the general response to the third generation Transporter must have warmed the cockles of VW's heart. *Car and Driver* cooed that what was, "draped over the revised chassis" was "one of the handsomer bodies ever tailored for a van". They then proceeded to marvel at the "15 per cent increase in the Vanagon's interior volume" and the "40 per cent improvement in rear luggage space".

Above: *The Range-Topping Caravelle Carat was a product of the mid-1980s. Roof mounted air conditioning, cruise control and auxiliary under-floor heating were some of the model's up-market attributes.*

Road and Track, noted the air-cooled engine's reputation for being noisy, but found it to be "so well insulated now that it's very subdued inside", and "especially competent on a miserable unpaved road". When *Motor Trend* named the Transporter their 'van of the year', they eulogised that the "Vanagon is one of the best utilitarian vehicles ever to take to the highway. Its efficient use of space, attention to ride comfort and sedan-like handling, position it as the new high mark the industry must strive to equal". Even before VW launched the third generation Transporter with an air-cooled engine, most would have acknowledged that the days of the what was basically Porsche's classic flat-four were numbered.

45

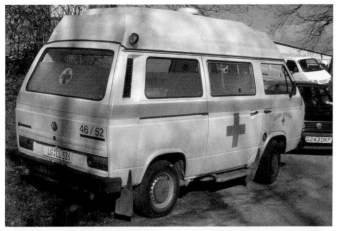

Top Left: *The later Water-Cooled version of the T25 Ambulance.*

Middle Left: *Westfalia's popular 'Joker' conversion based on the T25.*

Bottom Left: *The T25 Auto-sleeper conversion, continuing the long line of motor caravans based on the Transporter.*

Not only were the advances in diesel engine technology something of a threat, but also thanks to the turmoil of fuel shortages and escalating prices, potential purchasers were expecting a certain degree of economy out of their vehicle. If thrift wasn't a consideration, then performance certainly would be and while a Porsche 911 air-cooled engine offered just that, the two-litre VW lump didn't. Figures of 17 mpg were banded about, not only by the critical, but also at least in passing by less than wise gurus at Volkswagen Towers!

The anomaly of producing just one air-cooled engine, or worse still, two variations on the theme for one vehicle, possibly overlooked by Herr Schmücker in 1975 when the Beetle was still hanging on in there, just didn't make economic sense for Volkswagen. Thus, to wails of anguish from VW's loyal air-cooled followers, it was announced that water was to replace air in the petrol engine van. A low-key and somewhat under-powered diesel engine had been offered alongside the air-cooled range since September 1980.

However, there was still an anomaly, for this was no borrowed unit from one of the larger cars in the range, but a special 'wasserboxer', so still very much an expensive one-off!

In one of the numerous glossy publications churned out by Volkswagen's Public Relations department, on this occasion entitled "An Idea that made History" and published in 1991, the spin merchants added their particular twist to the tale. For the year 1982 they wrote the following entry. "The Transporter was now fitted with the newly developed water-cooled boxer engines … Consequently all Volkswagens with the exception of the Beetle had water-cooled engines. This was the conclusion of the technical re-structuring".

First out of the can, as far as a new direction was concerned, was a diesel engine borrowed from the Golf. Such was its low profile that Volkswagen doesn't even mention it in the countless reviews of the decades they publish. To squeeze the 1.6 into the Transporter, the in-line four was tilted at a 50° angle. For rather obvious reasons, the diesel had an extra grille at the front and sported a 'D' badge at the rear.

In the Volkswagen Golf, the diesel engine produced 50bhp, but this was nibbled away to 46bhp in the Type 25. Fuel consumption was hardly stunning at between 22 and 26mpg, perhaps something to do with a kerb weight increased by around 100kg to 1510kg.

September 1982 saw the arrival of the 'Wasserboxer', 1.9-litre engine, available in two variants. The base option had a single carb and produced 60bhp at 3,700rpm. That 78bhp was achieved at 4,400rpm was due mainly to a Pierburg downdraught two-stage carburettor. Such was the hullabaloo surrounding the engine's appearance that the brochure people went to the trouble of producing literature specifically proclaiming the "New water-cooled engine". Under a heading of, "such a super-duper new water-cooled engine", the copywriter sparkled, "The new ... water-cooled engine substantially improves fuel consumption and performance. While it increases engine life ... delivering up to 10 per cent more output ... it improves acceleration from 0-100km/h by a staggering 23 per cent. Making it more responsive. The installation of a new carburettor ... with electrical and coolant preheating, helps reduce fuel consumption by 14 per cent... A sophisticated thermostat cooling circuit controls water temperature even in the hottest or coldest conditions, prolonging engine life. While the electronic ignition system significantly reduces maintenance. More important, engine life is increased, while engine noise is reduced by a comfortable three decibels...."

Press reaction to the Wasserboxer was extremely positive, and this can be illustrated by the two quotations that follow.

For instance, the *Motor Manual* proclaimed that "more than ever, it makes the Transporters the Mercedes of the light van class ... inside its so smooth, you'd honestly be pushing to say it wasn't a six, rather than a four".

Meanwhile, the magazine *Road and Track* broke the rules, shouting about the new Transporter's "50 per cent reduction in noise levels" and the '19 per cent improvement in fuel economy". "The new engine's power, flexibility, economy and quietness are delightful and give the VW van a level of performance that is commensurate with its design", they concluded.

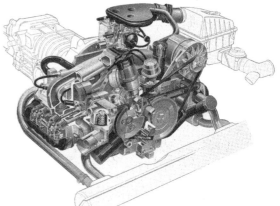

Top, Middle and Bottom Right: *Outwardly virtually unchanged, the brochure producers resorted to a flash to sell the new engines on the Transporter (top). The 60bhp petrol engine (middle) and the Diesel unit (bottom) were illustrated in cutaway form.*

In 1984, for the 1985 model year, a 90bhp fuel-injected engine was added, although initially only available in the special edition Caravelle Carat, where it was linked to a five-speed box. However, for the 1986 model year, this engine became available across the range, while computer-controlled, fuel-injection raised output to 95bhp. Hot on the heels of this development was a 2.1-litre fuel-injected engine, boasting a meaningful 112bhp. August 1985 also saw a new diesel engine emerge, this time a 1.6-litre turbo-charged terror, with Bosch fuel-injection, capable of producing 70bhp. In 1987, the non-turbo diesel received a boost up to 1.7-litres. In 1989 the 2.1-litre offering was dropped, the norm becoming a fuel-injected engine with a regulated catalytic converter and 92bhp at its disposal. If the multifarious array of engines was now far removed from the original 'box on wheels' concept, so too was the model range by the mid- to late -1980s, factors that make it questionable whether the water-

Above: *Illustrated elsewhere, but blatantly obvious on this Double-Cab Pickup, the additional, lower grille always indicates a T25 which has been fitted with a water-cooled engine.*

cooled Transporters should even be included in what is essentially a history of the evolution of the range outlined in Chapter Three.

The key to the shift away from what had been the planned or actual pattern for over 30-years, was the decision to re-brand the commercial vehicle products in September 1983. What had once been the Panelvan and Kombi became the Transporter, while the more upmarket Microbus offerings were labelled as the Caravelle, a term already used for special editions, and available at 'C', 'CL', and 'GL' levels of trim, in line with Golfs, Polos and Passats of the time.

Before VW re-branded the Transporter package, they had joined the limited edition game with a seven-seater Caravelle, which featured two-tone paint and chromed bumpers. Internally, luxurious armrests were provided for each seat, which in turn were both better padded and upholstered, whilst the refinements also included deep-pile carpets and a more up-market headlining. The dashboard was no longer just available in black, while storage compartments multiplied. This was in September 1981, but during 1982 Volkswagen did it again, when they offered a 'Tone in Tune' special, featuring Pewter Grey paint and a luxurious interior, carefully colour co-ordinated in black, silver and grey.

As a result of the re-branding exercise, there came a model that was even better appointed than the GL, but having the unfortunate name, of the Caravelle Carat. Such models were recognisable externally by their alloy wheels, additional body trim and twin rectangular headlights. At its launch, the first Carat model featured swivel seats centrally, the superfluous luxury of armrests, velour upholstery, better carpeting and at long last, a radio cassette as standard.

Volkswagen were happy to describe the Carat as an 'executive people carrier', which was targeted at either businesses who required an upmarket bus in which to ferry VIPs, or towards the larger family who wanted a luxury motor. The problem was one of price, as the tag headed increasingly close to the £20,000 mark. *Autocar* tested one in 1989. "Going some way towards justifying the elevated price tag is a plush interior with six armchair-like seats and thick pile carpeting. The outside is distinguished by alloy wheels with beefy tyres, lowered suspension, a metallic paint finish … tinted glass and a small chin spoiler. The specification includes central locking, electric front windows and power steering, but if you want the automatic gearbox, towbar, air conditioning, four-speaker Blaupunkt radio cassette and anti-lock brakes, as fitted to our test car, the price rockets to a staggering £23,973".

Below: *The 4x4 Syncro was launched in February 1985. "The nerve-centre of syncro technology is a viscous coupling which automatically monitors and controls the drive to the front wheels", explained a copywriter.*

To compliment the luxury game, VW also offered the four-wheel-drive story and in some instances combined the two! In the mid-1980s VW recalled their second generation experiments with four-wheel-drive and launched themselves into their own unique 'Synchro' world. The arrangement was developed by Steyr-Daimler-Puch, from the successful Ferguson system and meant that four-wheel drive only engaged when traction was lost through the rear wheels. As loss of grip was detected, the viscous front coupling/front differential locked up, enabling additional drive to the front wheels, automatically. Better still, on really rough terrain, the differential lock could be handled manually, if so desired.

Initially, available only coupled to the 1.9-litre, 78bhp carburettor engine, by late 1986, 'Synchro' had hit the big-time and was offered with the 112bhp 2.1-litre engine, as well as the diesel combinations. *Autocar*'s verdict was that for "someone requiring its particular combination of off-road and people carrying abilities, it may look to be a bargain …". However, the "Caravelle Synchro drives more like a van than a car, thanks to its rather ponderous gear-change, low-geared steering and lack of stability at higher speeds". Volkswagen played with a proper off-road version of the Synchro concept, adding 16" wheels, special shock absorbers, reinforced final drive and a stronger braking system. The body was reinforced and included larger wheel cutouts encased in plastic trim.

The water-cooled era of Type 25 production was typified by diversity. From the simple 1984 sunroof option in the Panelvan, via US demands for automatic options, to something as complex as the Tristar, which was a Carat-style luxury version of the double-cab Pickup, complete with Synchro, it was on offer. Cruise control arrived in 1986, ABS the following year, double headlamps popped up for all in 1989. Need more be said!

By the time that Volkswagen celebrated the official 40th anniversary of the Transporter on 8th March 1990, 6.7-million examples had been built primarily at Hanover, covering three generations. However, the writing was on the wall for the third, as in September the T4 was launched, a vehicle with both its engine and driving wheels at the front. So it is time for us to bid *adieu* and wait 10-years or so, before adding details of what might be another landmark vehicle.

Top, Middle and Bottom Left: *During 1989, all models received twin-square front lights, as illustrated on VWs promotional shot of the 'Coach' (Top) and the 'Bus' (Centre). The arrival of the T4 in August 1990 (Bottom) heralded the end of rear-engined VWs.*

CAMPING IT UP

The observer of any of the three generations of Volkswagen's Transporter cannot have failed to notice camper options in profusion, but in this volume, unless captions have been read and digested, not a word concerning their existence has appeared. The reasoning is simple; as for many years Volkswagen had no direct links with such vehicles, although eventually a loose partnership was established with the camping speciality firm of Westfalia. Here in Britain, a tacit acknowledgement of the familiar name of Devon took the story a stage further, but it was only in the years of diversity that VW themselves donned shorts and sleeping bags to produce an official VW Camper.

Throughout the book, campers are depicted and described in the captions. Their presence in the Transporter story is recalled here. By the 1930s the firm of Westfalia, so named due to its location in the State of North Rhine-Westfalia, had become a leading producer of caravans and camping trailers. Inevitably, like many German firms, Hitler's war took its toll and Westfalia was no exception.

Above: *The earliest British market-leader was Lisburne Garage of Torquay, aided by the invaluable skills of the long-established cabinet-making firm, J.P. White, based in nearby Sidmouth. Their 'Devon' range utilised either Kombis or Microbuses. The vehicle illustrated dates from the autumn of 1962 and is painted in Beige Grey over Sealing Wax Red.*

However, by 1947, they had rebuilt sufficiently to show their first all steel-plate caravan. The economic situation ensured that sales were ponderously slow, so when Volkswagen announced the arrival of the Transporter, the resourceful company saw a way of extending the provenance of the already versatile Kombi.

In April 1951, Westfalia launched their 'Camping Box'; essentially removable boxes, which provided drawers for sufficient essentials for a weekend away and doubled as a bed, thanks to the provision of comfortable cushions. Extras included a wooden cabinet with roll-down door, which (though not long enough to allow clothes to hang), doubled as a wardrobe. Washing facilities hung onto the rear of the Transporter's two side doors, while cooking was accomplished via a spirit or petrol-burning stove.

Above: *The Devon Moonraker, complete with Double Top Elevating Roof.*

Sales of Westfalia's Camping Box were initially slow, taking until 1958 for the 1000th such to be sold and only then when accompanied by the paraphernalia of a full-length striped awning and a hinged-roof-flap. Both dated from 1952 but a bar with 10-cocktail glasses, plus a chemical loo were 1954 additions. By 1960, the Transporter had made its debut as an official vehicle, being included in brochures and other literature. As such, it had a special interior including insulation, a water-tank, storage cupboards and the luxury of curtains!

By 1960, other names had started to jump on the bandwagon, invariably offering less expensive 'conversions'. In Britain, the first Devon models, courtesy of Lisburne Garage of Torquay and J.P. White cabinet-makers of Sidmouth had appeared in 1957, while Leeds-based Moortown leapt in with the Autohome at the start of the 1960s. Other names included Dormobile, Danbury, and Peter Pitt (later Canterbury Pitt).

Throughout the 1960s, Westfalia added variation to the theme. A polyester-folding roof appeared in 1963, a roof-storage area and refrigerator cropped up three-years later. In March 1968, Westfalia celebrated production of the 30,000th camper to be built, but with the Bay as base for an outdoor home, production escalated beyond belief. 50,000 had been made by May 1969 and 100,000 by the end of 1971, when Westfalia were building 125 campers every day. Sadly, the oil crisis of the mid-1970s halted further expansion. Westfalia promoted the Helsinki and Berlin models until the arrival of the T25, when they launched the Joker range, which included all sorts of goodies like swivel front seats. At the time of writing a **Nostalgia Road** book on camper vans is in the course of preparation.